YOU CAN HAVE MORE THAN MUSIC

Practical Helps for Planning, Directing, Leading, and Strengthening the Adult Choir

Jean Anderson

Abingdon Press

ACKNOWLEDGMENTS

I want to thank all the singers who have been part of choirs and ensembles I have directed through the years. Their willingness to participate, their understanding, their love—even as I searched for a way to make everything work—made all the difference.

To Barbara and Bob Deal I say "thank you" from the bottom of my heart—to Barbara for her unwavering belief in me and the value of this book; to Bob for his strong support of my sharing my experience; to both of them for their unconditional love.

GJA

To my mother, Claudia,
who made sure there was
music in my life.

CONTENTS

YOU CAN HAVE MORE THAN MUSIC

Copyright © 1990 by Abingdon Press

Library of Congress Cataloging-in-Publication Data

Anderson, G. Jean.
    You can have more than music : practical helps for planning,
      directing, leading, and strengthening the adult choir /
      G. Jean Anderson.
      p.   cm. — (Called to serve)
    ISBN 0-687-04607-6 (paper : alkaline)
    1. Church music.   2. Choirs (Music) I. Title. II. Series.
MT88.A57   1990
   264 ' .2 '0683—dc20

                                    90-45569
                                            CIP
                                            MN

Scripture quotations noted JBP are from *The New Testament in Modern English*, by J. B. Phillips. Copyright © 1958, 1959, 1960, 1972.

Scripture quotations noted KJV are from the King James Version of the Bible.

Scripture quotations noted NIV are taken from the *Holy Bible: New International Version*. Copyright © 1973, 1978, 1984 by the International Bible Society. Used by permission of Zondervan Bible Publishers.

Hymnal indexes on p. 25 are from *The United Methodist Hymnal*. Copyright © 1989 by The United Methodist Publishing House.

Manufactured in the United States of America

INTRODUCTION

In the Gospel of Luke (12:31) we are advised that we should seek first the kingdom of God and that everything else we're looking for will follow. This book has grown out of my experience in attempting to take this advice to heart in working with church choirs. While any choral group's purpose certainly is to make music, I've found that real success for the choir has its roots in mutual caring and support among choir members. When there is an atmosphere of unconditional love (and I submit that this applies universally), the church choir can succeed, no matter the size of the group. As in anything else, seeking God's kingdom of love *first* allows us to discover treasures far beyond any benefits we have contemplated. We can have much more than the music.

I have always lived in awe of music, particularly its ability to speak directly to the heart. Robert Browning wrote, "Would you have your songs endure? Build on the human heart." Music is truly a divine international language; when it sings with love, the effect is irresistible. Those of us who have felt called to serve as choir directors or choir members have a magnificent opportunity; with our songs we can assist the Christ to touch lives in a unique way. We can be willing to serve as channels for the voice of God.

The following is a song that also works well as a round. I know of at least one choir that sings it to begin each choir practice. It says best what I feel—that we sing only because God sings through us. We are God's instruments on earth. To love and to serve are the greatest privileges available to us. The choir that knows this will succeed.

PRAYER
A Four-Part Canon

G. Jean Anderson

Barbara Neighbors Deal

1. Voice of God, speak and sing;
2. Write Your mu-sic, let me bring
3. Words of love, notes of joy,
4. in Your world my voice em-ploy.

© Copyright 1990, AmaDeus Group

1. THE CHOIR AS WORSHIP LEADER

The most important function of the church choir is to perform music on Sunday morning, either as a group or by use of soloists. Performing lets the congregation see what the choir has been accomplishing at practice. As talented individuals the choir members can thereby entertain people in the church.

If you agree with the statements above, you might as well plan to read another book, because you won't be interested in what I have to say. I have no intention of making the choir seem unimportant, as I think it's a vital part of the Sunday worship service. However, it is important and vital because its members can serve as worship leaders, rather than act as performers. There is a big difference.

In most churches the choir sits in front of the congregation, in full view. The choir has the wonderful potential for helping to create an energetic service. By joyful enthusiasm, staying "tuned in" to the order of service, and bringing their full consciousness and attention to what is going on, choir members can set up a reciprocity of energy between the people up front (ministers, assisting staff, and the choir itself), and those people sitting in the pews.

I've often heard choir members voice such complaints as, "It was really hard to sing this morning; everybody out there seemed like they were asleep!" A choir member who feels this way is missing the point.

The choir is not there to sing to anybody, but to lead and assist the congregation in worship through music. There isn't any we and them on Sunday morning—or there should not be—it's all us.

The choir usually looks different, easily distinguishable, with its robes or other type of uniform, but it is part of the congregation even though it sits in a special place. When the hymns are sung, the choir may be singing four part harmony while the rest of the congregation generally sings the melody—but singing—along with responsive readings and congregational prayers—is an activity in which everyone can participate. The choir members need to look at themselves as active leaders, not as performers who have been brought in to sing a couple of special numbers in the service, and therefore saving their energy and attention for those moments when they are performing.

The choir is made up of different types of people, just as is the congregation. The choir is a microcosm of the church membership. There are persons who can hardly wait to sing on Sunday morning; there are also those who are shy about being up front, and many who fall in between these two extremes. They have joined the choir because, presumably, they want to sing. Any choir that sees its primary role as performing and separates itself from the rest of the congregation is not carrying out the true function of a choir. It is not living up to its great potential for service. If the head of the finance committee and his or her fellow volunteers are concerned only with collecting money and not with people and their needs, the church probably will experience money problems.

Service is what choir participation is all about—service offered to the glory of God. When the choir members look at choir membership as an avenue of service, where God given talents and abilities can be put to use and shared, then they can give 100 percent all the time. They will not wait for the congregation to wake up before they begin to be excited about what they are doing.

When the minister or another person is speaking, reading scripture, or making announcements, choir members need to direct their full attention to that person. If the organist or pianist is playing a solo, their attention needs to be directed there. When everyone sings hymns or responses, the choir needs to be participating fully. This doesn't mean only that everyone is singing the music; it means that the entire choir sings with animation, with enthusiasm—joyfully, reverently, or in whatever spirit is appropriate. *Enthusiasm* is derived from a Greek word that means "God in us." Thus, the choir can help to *lead* the worship with enthusiasm.

The choir cannot depend on what they see in the congregation for energy. Rather, the choir's enthusiasm, love, and joy will be contagious and involve the rest of the congregation in that excitement. As the choir members sing anthems or special choir music, the listeners will accept the gift, take it in, and send back their own appreciation, love, and joy to the choir and accompanist. Then the choir is not only giving, it also is receiving.

Music adds unique beauty to a church service, whether it is instrumental or vocal, choir or solo. It is one of the loveliest gifts humankind has been given. The choir has the opportunity to contribute some of that beauty, by itself and with the congregation. All of us should take to heart Colossians 3:15-16 as we consider the role of the choir as worship leaders:

Let the peace of Christ guide all your decisions, for you were called to live as one united body; and always be thankful. Let the full richness of Christ's teaching find its home among you. Teach and advise one another wisely. Use psalms and hymns and Christian songs, singing God's praises from joyful hearts." (JBP)

2. GETTING TO KNOW YOU

Getting to Know You" could well be the theme song of the successful church choir. Success in this case means open, trusting, sharing and loving. A choir can sing the most demanding music, do a praiseworthy job technically, and still be unsuccessful in its personal relationships—in members knowing and trusting each other. The ideal, of course, is to have both: the choir members interact with each other in an open, loving way, and they also attain musical excellence. Is this possible? Especially in a volunteer choir, which may be very small? It is.

In a small group, the chances are that people already know each other at least somewhat; perhaps they are not close friends, but they sit together on Sunday and they rehearse together. Even though the group may be small, they might still have difficulty in being open to each other, or in feeling free to say what they really think and feel. The choir members' relationships with each other might be getting in the way of achieving oneness as a group. This possibility is much greater in a large group.

Harmony is essential, not only in the music, but among the singers of the music as well. I'm not suggesting that everybody needs to be in complete agreement on everything. There can be room for differences of opinion. But an atmosphere of love must be created so that every person knows that it's okay to be who they are. When each person knows that, it becomes okay for everybody else to be who they are.

We human beings tend to give the best of ourselves when we feel safe and loved. I think of this as giving of "ourSelves"—capital S for the highest and best that is in us. A church choir is no different from any other group in many ways. The choir is made up of individuals, each of whom brings his or her own talents, abilities, insecurities, and fears. All of us want to contribute; however, sometimes that unique contribution is not made. We hold back because we don't feel free to be who we are. In the choir, as in any group, a safe place needs to be created for people to contribute their best as individuals and as singers.

Choir members need to know that whatever else has happened in their lives during the week, when they arrive at choir practice they can leave all of it outside the practice room.

Choir practice is a place where members can know they will be accepted as a valuable part of the whole and appreciated for the unique contribution each person makes in terms of singing and personality; they need not bring their problems to choir practice. One way to help this happen is five or ten minutes before the scheduled conclusion of the rehearsal, have the entire group form a circle. This is an opportunity to express thanks for support, requests for prayer, and to share what is happening in their lives. Many singers have told me that at the end of rehearsal they feel buoyed, supported, encouraged, and inspired to the point of being able to see solutions and alternatives to some of their problems.

The kind of loving atmosphere described above cannot be developed unless everyone is willing to set aside their judgements for the duration of the rehearsal. The choir practice can be a time of unconditional love for all those involved—both choir members and the director. Singers need to raise their hearts just as they raise their voices as children of God, singing to God's glory and seeing each other as part of the Divine plan. As this love and caring is practiced, along with the music, week after week, a shift can occur in the consciousness of the choir members. They can truly begin to know and trust each other. Then the way is clear for everyone to contribute to one another as people who have come together to make music. They become successful.

The choir is a microcosm of the church. It stands to reason that it serves the choir to be together in social situations like potlucks, birthday celebrations, and setting aside time now and then—perhaps two or three times a year—to discuss goals and ideas. This need not be a dull and dry experience. Why not have dessert, coffee, tea, or punch and "kick back"? It is important to share these casual times. If the choir is really working on choir practice night, there isn't enough time for a lot of discussion and fellowship. People come to sing, and too much chatter will sabotage the rehearsal. Because it doesn't occur frequently, the planning night can be something people won't feel burdened by, and it has been my experience that a lot of good can come out of it—as well as a lot of fun.

So, regardless of the size of the choir—these same principles work whether the group is sixty or six—the essential element is love, just as it is in any successful church, again considering the definition of successful to be loving, caring, and sharing. The vocal success will flow from this. After all, our assignment here on earth is to love God and each other; music, no matter in what setting, always seems to make that easier. The choir need only be willing in order to accomplish the desired result. Once the willingness is present, we can be transformed by the renewing of our minds. The choir can bring the love that exists among its members to church on Sunday morning and give it away. And the miraculous quality of love is this: the more we give away, the more we have.

3. AT REHEARSAL

There are a few simple things that can make the difference between a choir rehearsal that leaves everyone feeling frazzled and frustrated—even though it has produced a good musical result—and a practice that sends choir members home feeling lifted, inspired, and beaming.

A Productive Practice Begins with Keeping Agreements.
If the group has agreed that rehearsal is to start at 7:00 P.M., it needs to start at 7:00. Don't wait for late arrivals. It is unfair to those who have showed up on time and it gives silent approval for people to be late. This ties in with another important rule that I feel should not be broken:

If You Don't Rehearse the Music at Choir Practice, You Don't Sing the Anthem on Sunday Morning.
When a choir member misses practice or arrives thirty or forty minutes into the rehearsal and the choir has completed polishing Sunday's anthem, it should mean that the individual does not sing that piece. There is no reason he or she can't sit with the choir, to participate in singing the rest of the service, such as other hymns and responses. But one person who hasn't practiced can make mistakes. He or she is unfamiliar with the changes the director might have made, and can sometimes foul up an otherwise well prepared anthem.

Many choirs have someone who has a great voice and is a good reader. Too often directors—especially if the choir is small—will allow that person to sing on Sunday after missing the rehearsal because they are so glad to have the additional vocal support. But again, this is unfair to those members who have practiced, and it sets an unfortunate precedent that the choir can eventually come to resent. A simple hymn sung in unison is a perfectly acceptable anthem when there are only a few at practice; the congregation will appreciate it and the choir will respect the decision.

Organize the Rehearsal Time.
To save valuable time during the rehearsal, have the music in an easily accessible place so that people can pick up copies as they come in. It works well to let the choir know the order in which pieces will be practiced. The director pre-sumably will have decided this before the practice begins, and can simply announce the order or write it on a blackboard. I prefer having it written so no time at all need be spent in going through it aloud, and choir members can begin to organize their music as soon as they arrive. Smooth transitions can then be made from completing work on one piece to commencing work on another, and it cuts down the talk time.

If the rehearsal lasts two hours or more, a short break (fifteen minutes at most) will probably be in order. It is a good idea to have any necessary announcements made just five or ten minutes before the break. Individuals who want to make announcements themselves should let that be known in advance, but the best plan is to have all announcements made by the choir president or the director. Again, it is important that everyone keep the agreement. It is disruptive to have people sharing information during the singing portion of choir practice, and too much talk will not make for a productive rehearsal.

Keep Announcements Brief and Avoid Discussion.
Name a contact person to whom the choir members can talk if they need more information. When there are decisions that need discussion, or if social gatherings or special events are being planned, a time other than choir practice needs to be designated.

Opening and Closing the Rehearsal.
A wonderful way to help the choir come into oneness of spirit as the rehearsal begins is to open with a moment of prayer. It is also good to end the rehearsal with a prayer or sharing circle.

Be sure to take into consideration the time needed for these activities as you plan the rehearsal so that the choir practice ends at the scheduled time, not ten or fifteen minutes later. If people want to stay around and visit with each other, they may, but keep the time agreement so that those who need to leave may do so.

Commitment Is the Foundation of a Successful Volunteer Choir.
Without commitment the choir cannot succeed. It needs to be very clear that when a singer joins the choir, he or she is expected to make a commitment to attend the rehearsals and to be there on time. I

cannot stress this point too strongly. Because it is difficult for some people to keep long-term commitments to activities as time consuming as choir membership, a good procedure is to divide the choir year. For example, if the choir rehearses September through June, the first commitment term might be September through December (encompassing Christmas music), while the second term is January through June. It is easier for some people to keep a commitment that lasts for only a few months rather than a year.

If someone must miss a practice, as in the case of illness or emergency, a phone call to the director, section leader, or choir president is a necessary courtesy. There are various possibilities in structuring this, but to simply not show up on choir practice night—or even to be late—is breaking the commitment. Any time a singer is absent the whole choir is affected; practice is not the same musically, or from the perspective of group dynamics.

The Choir Agrees to Commit.

At the beginning of this chapter I stated, "If the group has decided the time for rehearsal. . . ." It is important for the choir to take responsibility for the way it will work—making the agreements that will be the guidelines for its success. When the choir director has made all the rules—and decisions are made unilaterally—it shouldn't be surprising when singers resist; after all they have had nothing to say about the decisions. Often directors become frustrated at absences, lateness, and lack of cooperation, resorting to sarcasm and remarks that sting. This is always sad *and* self-defeating, and has no place in the volunteer choir. Such an attitude can be avoided by having the group make its own decisions and agreements. Obviously some things will have to be decided by the choir director, but as much as possible, the choir should actively participate in setting its own course.

4. TIME TO TALK

Choir practice time is for singing. The statement seems obvious, yet often choirs allow their precious rehearsal time to be consumed by too much talk. A choir—a microcosm of the church—occasionally needs to make decisions as a body. Unless all things are to be decided by the director, which really doesn't work with the volunteer choir, there needs to be a certain amount of time for exchange of ideas. Even if there are no weighty decisions to be made, the group needs time together for talking and listening to each other, to solve problems, and to build fellowship. That time is not during choir practice.

A choir meeting—a meeting apart from the usual choir practice—is a wonderful way to afford opportunity to deal with choir business, to celebrate birthdays and other good news, and to plan special events and programs. Most of all, it gives the choir members a chance to get better acquainted. If the rehearsal time is being used appropriately, there should not be time to visit, too.

Many choirs sabotage the choir practice by spending so much time talking in between each piece of music, or engaging in long group discussions on a variety of topics, that in a typical rehearsal it would be remarkable if they devoted a full hour to singing. But before we rush to condemn talking and visiting as undesirable, immature behavior for adults, let's remember that humans are social animals and it is natural and healthy for us to want to interact with each other. But we have not come to choir practice primarily to chat!

When the choir members know there will be time set aside for socializing, they more easily will agree to stay focused at rehearsal, and to use the choir practice time in the way it is meant to be used: for singing. Of course, a period of time will be spent before and after rehearsal in talking and visiting, but I cannot emphasize too strongly the importance of beginning and ending on time.

It is very helpful for choirs to elect a president. The choir president acts as an assistant to the choir director in non-music matters. These might include making announcements at choir practice when needed (no more than seven to eight minutes for this), taking phone calls from those who know they will be late or absent on rehearsal night, and doing other things that keep the choir director free to concentrate on the music. It is important for the president to be someone who knows how to delegate tasks; it is not necessary for that individual to do everything alone. The choir president is responsible for organizing the choir meetings and can ask people to assist in planning how that time together will be spent. The choir president also can serve as representative of the choir in church business.

I have always liked the idea of having a choir librarian. It is best for the director to appoint someone to this position—someone who is willing to serve and who is a good organizer. The librarian is responsible for keeping the music together and in good repair; the extent of duties will depend on how large the music library is.

If the choir is newly formed, it is good to start off on the right note by numbering each copy of sheet music, and creating a file system, showing the name of the composer(s), how many copies are in the library, and so forth. It is also helpful for the librarian to note the date the anthem is sung in the file system. This helps the director avoid too many repetitions of old favorites, and encourages recycling of the library.

When the library is already in existence—and perhaps extensive—this filing system should still be set up, though it will take more time. Of course, the choir librarian doesn't have to do everything alone; he or she can ask for assistance.

Many choirs keep their music in folders. Color coding the folders according to the tone of anthem (energetic and joyous, contemplative and worshipful), or by *type* of anthem (classical, spiritual, contemporary), can be helpful to both the director and the librarian. The folders may be stored in file drawers or boxes with the title, type, composer, and publisher clearly labelled on the tab. Another option is to have shelves built with the space of about the width of a ream of paper between the shelves. The file folders can then be labelled on the spine. Whatever storage system is used, I prefer to file music alphabetically by anthem name. A cross reference index by composer(s) name is also helpful to have.

Once the library is organized and the storage system established, it doesn't take much to keep things tidy and easy to find. The choir director and the choir will greatly appreciate an efficient librarian. For the right person, the satisfaction in this position is tremendous.

As in other suggestions I have made with regard to practical procedures, these are only just that—*suggestions*. A responsible librarian working with the director can establish the best arrangement for their particular situation.

The choir meeting is not about music, necessarily; it is possible that the sole purpose might be a social one. It might be held at the church, if there is a room that is the right size, without being austere. It might be at someone's home, if that is agreeable and feels comfortable for everybody. It can be a potluck or a dessert and coffee/tea/punch evening. Choir members who do the planning undoubtedly will have suggestions from the group and can proceed accordingly. Whatever the arrangements, they should be communicated clearly to the choir during the period for announcements. If more than one or two questions are asked, request that the choir members talk to the president *after* practice, as such discussions are exactly what we want to eliminate from the singing time. Choir meetings can be held as often as the group wants to have them, but my experience has shown that meeting once every six to eight weeks is beneficial without being a burden on anyone.

Choirs sometimes like to begin in September—after summer is over—with a choir retreat. The choir can get away from familiar surroundings and sing through the music that the director has chosen, or is considering, for use during the coming months. This also is an excellent time for new members to come into the choir and get acquainted, as there is time for one-to-one chats.

The choir meeting is a wonderful time to listen to good music—either music that has been sung by the choir, or is presently being learned, or will be learned in the future. Often at Christmas time it's fun to have a sing-along *Messiah,* and this also can be done with any choral music. Put on the tape or recording, give everybody a copy of the score, and celebrate!

The most important thing to keep in mind is that the choir must "own" their agreements on everything from the length of the rehearsal to how many months per year they will practice. To be successful, the volunteer choir needs to participate in setting its guidelines and agreeing to them. In addition, choirs are not unique in that members will not be willing to make and keep a commitment to an organization that does not allow them to feel that they make a difference by belonging to it. The choir director, of course, must take overall responsibility for the choir and its function in the church, but when the singers understand that each member makes a one-of-a-kind contribution, then their roles as worship leaders become meaningful and fulfilling to them. Their joy and enthusiasm are contagious.

The spiritual glue that holds the successful volunteer choir together is the members' caring for each other and for the choir itself. The choir meeting is an important tool to help create a strong bond of love in the choir and it lets the choir practice be what it is meant to be.

5. NEW CHOIR? NEW DIRECTOR?

If you are not a choir director and have agreed to organize a choir in a church that has not had one before, then you probably feel a little like Isaiah: "Here am I, Lord, send me!" The enthusiasm is sincere and you want to serve, but after you have committed yourself there is nagging doubt about whether it will be possible. You wonder why you ever said yes in the first place. Maybe you have never directed any group, but perhaps you play the piano (a little or a lot), or the guitar (even just chords), and with these credentials you find that you are the person in the church who knows more about music than anyone else. For this reason you are the one who has been asked to put together a choir.

The most important thing for you to remember is: Don't panic! You can do what has been asked. Whether you end up directing the choir for many years—as a friend of mine has done under similar circumstances—or whether you simply do the ini-

tial organizing and work with the choir for a short time until someone else takes over as director, there are ways to keep your agreement to form a group of singers. And you can feel good about it while it's happening.

Don't be afraid to admit that you are not experienced. Admit that you are nervous about the undertaking and be willing to open yourself to Divine direction. Be willing to listen to the suggestions of others, whether or not you take them. Be willing to work with the people who are interested in being in the choir, to support them and accept their support. You can give it your best effort. Obviously, the people who asked you to undertake this project believe you have the ability or they would not have asked you. You have a love of music; you recognize that this is one way you can use your talent and serve. Don't forget that others will be encouraging and supportive of you; you are not alone. "I can do all things through Christ which strengtheneth me" (Philippians 4:13, KJV)—even direct a choir!

I believe that the main purpose of the church choir is to serve as worship leader, to assist the congregation in singing, and to provide whatever additional vocal music is desired within the framework of the church service to enrich the worship of the congregation. While the smaller church choir is made up of volunteers, and singers will not be auditioned, it is important for people interested in joining the choir to be able to match tones, carry a tune, and to have a willingness to make a commitment to the choir and grow in musicianship.

It is not necessary that everyone be able to read music, as those who do read will lead the way for those who do not. However, I do not think it is a good idea to invite one and all to participate with the primary intention of filling seats. Some basic musicianship, or the willingness to learn it, is necessary. If you fail to say what you expect in the beginning, and you stay on as director, you will have to deal with the resulting unsatisfactory situation later on. So why not be clear about requirements for choir membership from the start?

If individuals do not know what part they sing most comfortably—soprano, alto, tenor or bass—it is a fairly simple thing to discover through voice testing.

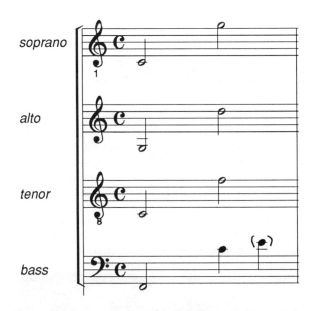

Of course, individuals may have wider or narrower ranges, according to ability. Have the person sing a piece he or she knows well, such as a hymn, "America," or some nursery rhyme. Listen to the quality of the voice, the color, the range the person is able to manage, and so forth. With some voices it will be easy to determine whether they sing a high or low part; in cases where it is not clear, assign the person to a section and let him or her try it out for a while. If an alto is attempting to sing soprano, she will realize in a short time that it just isn't comfortable and she can move into the appropriate section. If people are nervous about singing in front of the whole group in these efforts to place them, have them meet with you one at a time. It is important that the singers realize early that the choir is a safe place, and that they are going to be loved unconditionally by you as the director, and by the other singers. Voice testing can be conducted in a way that is non-threatening when the director approaches it with sincere caring and love.

Once the sections are established it is time to start singing. However, in the event that there are not the vocal resources to have soprano, alto, tenor, and bass, it is perfectly all right. Take people as you find them and see what can be accomplished. Begin with what is comfortable musically. This may be a simple hymn each Sunday for a time; there is nothing wrong with using a soloist on alternate verses while the choir hums. Or use the women and men on alternate verses. Let the organ or piano play a verse alone. Sing in unison. These procedures can be very effective and aren't too taxing on anyone. The congregation will appreciate what the group does, both as individuals and collectively. Meanwhile, the choir will be fulfilling its role as worship leader, enhancing the times of praise, contemplation, or prayer through its music. Each success will allow the choir to grow in confidence and fellowship. As this joy is reflected in the choir members, new singers will be attracted to the group. As the size of the choir increases and additional voices are added, more challenging music can be tackled.

It is important for the director to be aware of the tremendous impact he or she can have in organizing a new choir. If the director has a positive attitude and refuses to become discouraged, can keep a sense of humor, is eager to assist the choir in fulfilling its role as worship leader, then these things will go a long way toward ensuring the initial success of the choir. There will be immediate wins, when the singers feel proud of themselves for doing a good job, even though the choir might be few in number. The attitude of the director will be passed on to the people in the choir, and when there is a belief that "We can do it!," success is assured (Mark 11:24). The bonding of choir members is essential, not necessarily for musical accomplishment—there are many choirs that sing well technically but which have no real affection for each other. These choirs therefore fail in terms of serving as worship leaders because they provide nothing to the congregation beyond good performances.

Any person who is to serve as a worship leader should, of course, lead. When the choir members know and care about each other, their caring and warmth reaches into the rest of the church and comes back in the form of acknowledgment and appreciation. The choir is no different from any other group or setting, for in any case "the greatest of these is love" (1 Corinthians 13:13b, NIV). The choir's love for each other, for the music, and for the shared experience of worship leads the entire congregation into an experience of God's love and presence.

6. WHEN TWO OR THREE AGREE

If the choir is a microcosm of the church, it makes sense to do everything possible to strengthen choir fellowship and commitment. The most successful volunteer groups are the ones in which people know each other well and feel comfortable together.

Many groups can sing well, but they are not always what I consider successful in terms of human relationships, and they often have trouble in getting members to commit to the choir. Let's look at *commitment* for a moment.

Choir commitment means that the choir members agree (give their word) to attend rehearsals and to be present on Sunday mornings to sing in the choir during the church service. It means being on time to rehearsals and Sunday warm-up and practice. These two things are basic and are certainly not outrageous demands for the director to make. The choir commitment means that a singer's time is already spoken for on rehearsal night, that he/she is not available for other activities. This can be very freeing in that a choir member doesn't even have to think twice about doing anything else on that night; TV programs, sports events, movies, lethargy, and all other things that are part of living cannot distract us when we are *committed*. Of course, many choir members have spouses and children and occasionally there are bound to be times when family circumstances will require that someone must be at home or at a school event. These are the times when a choir member needs to fulfill his/her role as committed partner or committed parent. I am not referring to these occasions.

However, from week to week there are certain to be evenings when we are tired, frustrated, or discouraged and spectator amusements can be very appealing. But when we have made a commitment to bring ourselves and our voices to choir practice, we can keep our agreement, knowing we can be restored by the beauty and joy of the music, encouraged by loving friends, supported by God's strength. I have often told choirs that they can check their "stuff" (worries, anxieties, problems) at the door when they come in to rehearsal. If, after the practice is over, they want to pick it up and take it home with them, it will still be there.

Each of us has a unique contribution to make in the world, in the church, and in the choir—nobody else can do anything just the way we do it. Each choir member is valuable; it matters if one of us does not show up for rehearsal, and not only with regard to the musical balance. The group dynamics are simply not the same without any one of us. It is obvious that the personal relationships of the choir need to be remarkably supportive if someone is going to pass up the many activities and entertainments available. Why would anybody want to commit to being with the choir?

If you knew a place where people always welcomed you, put you at ease, accepted you just as you are, gave you understanding and support through every difficult time, and most of all, where people loved you, wouldn't you want to be with them? The choir that makes sharing the love of Christ its first goal will not fail to have enough members who in turn share their God-given talents and love with the congregation.

How do we share the love we know as God's children? We have sincere interest in the well-being of others, we encourage each other, and we celebrate significant occasions such as birthdays. Sometimes we get together for no reason other than the fact that we care about each other. We are like a family. The constant, palpable presence of love is the most drawing power in the world and the choir that creates the feeling of unconditional love will succeed. Keeping a commitment to that type of choir is not a burden; it is a joy. A miraculous result is that out of the mutual caring can come musical excellence.

The sense of fellowship, a bond of love, the sense of being One in Christ is what can make even the smallest volunteer choir successful, just as it can a large semi-professional choir—just as it can make a church the place people want to be on Sunday morning.

What a privilege it is to be able to sing God's praise! Composers throughout history have been inspired by the amazing example of Jesus and have left us a legacy of beautiful music with which to commemorate that unique life. Surely one of the places that commemoration needs to take place is the choir. There must be an atmosphere of unconditional love for everyone and a recognition of each person's worth first as a human being, then as a choir member. When there is such acceptance and love, there will be no shortage of singers; people will be drawn to the choir because they see Christ's love made manifest. They will gladly commit their time and talent to be a part of that organization. Truly blessed is the church with such a choir.

7. IN THE BEGINNING . . .

If you have agreed to become the choir director for your church, the chances are you know the rudiments of music even though your experience as a choral director is perhaps limited or nil. Perhaps you have played guitar or have a nodding acquaintance with the piano. In any case if you know how to count to four and if you have a real interest in working with a choir, you can provide the leadership needed for a successful group. I cannot say this too often or too strongly: The most important thing is love. A choir in which the singers and director genuinely care about each other provides the atmosphere for joyful learning together. Out of the awareness of and thankfulness for God's gift of love and music can come good singing. This does not necessarily work in reverse order. It is a little like seeking the Kingdom—once we direct ourselves to that, everything begins to fall into place. Having accepted the challenge and being conscious of creating an atmosphere of unconditional love, how do you go about the basics of actually conducting the choir?

It is important to allow singers an opportunity to warm up their voices when they arrive for practice. This can be a unifying time, when people begin to get into the rehearsal by doing a few simple vocal exercises. I like to take a light approach to warm-ups because many people do not relish the idea of exercise of any kind. Who says warm ups can't be fun as well as productive and helpful? Here are some basic ones:

1. Starting on G and using the syllable "ha"—

Ha Ha Ha Ha Ha Ha Ha Ha Ha Ha

Ha Ha Ha Ha Ha Ha Ha Ha Ha Ha *etc.*

Repeat and raise one-half step each time. (I usually go as high as a high G for sopranos and tenors; altos and basses may drop out when/if it becomes uncomfortable.)

2. Do an arpeggio (broken chord) on "me" (and continue to raise the key as above).

Me_____ Me _____ *etc.*

3. Sing an arpeggio on "me" and change to "ah" to get a little fancier.

Me _____ Ah _____ *etc.*

4. Use "ho" for this one—(very good at Christmas!).

Ho Ho Ho Ho Ho Ho Ho Ho Ho Ho

Ho Ho Ho Ho Ho Ho Ho Ho Ho Ho *etc.*

Have singers place a hand on the diaphragm muscle just above the stomach to be conscious of breathing from there rather than from the throat. If breathing correctly, they can see the hand move in and out. (An alternative: Use the five vowel sounds with the above.)

Repeat the above note progression using

Ha Ha Ha Ha Ha
He He He He He
Ho Ho Ho Ho Ho
Hu Hu Hu Hu Hu

5. Singing "moo," begin with basses on C, add tenors on G five notes above. Have altos sing middle C and sopranos an E three notes above. Ask singers to hold the notes, breathing when necessary, keeping the tone going. Have them listen to each other's voices producing the chord, concentrating on blending. Sometimes I ask them to visualize their individual notes converging when they reach the director, blending into one rich sound. To me, this is a wonderful picture of what the choir is — many separate and distinct individuals, each with his or her own interesting personality and physical characteristics, joining together to create *one* entity, a church choir. As one the choir raises its voice to praise and pray.

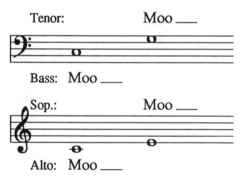

Every few minutes, have the group break the sound and repeat the warm-up a half step higher. Use this as many times as you choose until you begin to hear an improvement in the blend. If you do not immediately hear it, do not be discouraged. Remember this is a new choir; these things are very likely new to them and might take some getting used to. Try to remember to keep it light, do not lose your sense of humor and enjoy all of it along with the singers. You are learning together. Keep in mind that they are looking to you for direction, as well as support and encouragement. Be generous (but honest) in praising them for their effort.

In the beginning, probably seven or eight minutes is enough time for warm-ups. As the choir improves and begins to see for themselves the value of the procedure, you might decide to spend the first fifteen minutes of the rehearsal on warming up their voices. Again, I like to approach these exercises just as a basketball team does the pre-game time: they shoot a few baskets, practice passing and running, getting themselves ready. It would be unthinkable for a professional singer to walk out onto the stage to give a concert without having spent a period warming up the voice. While we as choir members might not be giving a performance for the public or our congregation each time we practice, we are preparing ourselves to sing for God, to give back something of what we have been given, and it needs to be the best we have to offer.

Create your own warm ups; there is no magic to it. After you have been together for awhile, all of you will begin to discover which things serve best. You might want to create some that deal with particular problems you encounter in singing certain anthems. At any rate, let the voices have a chance to get ready to sing before plunging into the rehearsal. A suggestion: Just as we give the voices a little limbering up before practicing choir music, I think the director needs to arrive at least fifteen to twenty minutes early on choir night in order to limber up and get organized. I prefer to have the rehearsal already planned in my mind or better yet, on paper, before arriving. I like to have the pieces arranged in the order we will sing them, and in general have a good idea of what the rehearsal is going to look like. Those extra minutes beforehand can be valuable to my peace of mind so that I don't feel scattered. If you choose to have a centering prayer before singing, that is wonderful. Keep it brief—people are there to sing.

I have not spent a lot of time on vocal placement, support, projection of the voice, or any other of the many aspects of singing. I have chosen not to because I do not consider myself a voice teacher. This section is intended as a helpful tool primarily for the person who has not previously conducted a choir and who is looking for assistance in the steps to get started. There are many books, magazines, and journals available that deal with these topics and others in great detail, which can often be found in the local library. I encourage the director who wants to expand his or her expertise with regard to these aspects of singing (which can be passed on to the choir) to spend some time researching the finer points.

For the director who is seeking the way for the choir to take its place as a prime contributor to the worship service—to become worship leaders—I hope the helpful hints in this chapter and the next will start you on your way.

8. I CAN DO ALL THINGS THROUGH CHRIST

The basic information provided at the beginning of any piece of music is the key signature and rhythm. In simplest terms this means what key the piece is in and how it is counted. I have had choir singers ask me, "How will I know to sing a sharp or a flat at the right place?" Fortunately for us, God has taken care of that problem; we don't need to worry about the fact that there might be two or three sharps or flats in the key. No adjustments are needed in the voice and most of the time we do not even have to be concerned about the key in which we are singing.

Once in a while there will be an "accidental," an altered note changed from what the key calls for, and we will have to pay attention to that. But generally speaking, we can feel that shift and need not be concerned with the intellectual process at all. Anyone using the Divine instrument (our human voice) does not have to worry about things the pianist or other instrumentalist must wrestle with. Once we are in the appropriate key—the tonality—we can go our merry way, singing and making a "joyful noise." Of course, there are untold numbers of books on the theory of music, offering a general education in reading music, but the truth is it is not necessary to have all that information in order to direct a choir. I do, however, encourage neophyte choir directors to explore this field in order to expand their own knowledge and that of their choirs. The good news for singers is that once the tonality is established from the piano or organ, we have our musical bearings; the internal, mysterious workings of ourselves as God's creations allow us to have a feel for the music. We must then learn the notes and rhythm that express the idea the composer had in mind in writing the piece.

For the person who has not had experience in directing a choir, beating time can be intimidating, but it doesn't have to be. Again, there is nothing magical about how it is done. The time indications at the beginning of a piece of music (2/4, 3/4, 4/4, 6/8) are very easy to comprehend, even for those who share my feelings of inadequacy about mathematics.

The top number in the time indication tells how many beats are in each measure. The bottom number tells what kind of note (whole , half , quarter , eighth) receives one beat. For example, "Joy to the World" is written in 2/4 time:

Joy to the World

```
1. Joy    to  the  world,  the  Lord  is   come!
2. Joy    to  the  world,  the  Sav - ior  reigns!
3. No   more let  sins   and  sor - rows  grow,
4. He  rules the  world  with truth and   grace,
```

There are two beats to each measure, a quarter note receives one beat. (A logical conclusion: If a quarter note receives 1 beat, a half note ( ) would receive two beats, an eighth ( ) note 1/2 beat, and so forth.)

Another example: "We Gather Together" has a marking of 3/4—three beats to a measure, a quarter note ( ) has one beat. "It Came upon the Midnight Clear" is in 6/8—six beats in a measure, an eighth note ( ) receives one beat, a quarter note has two beats. Most likely this material a person with some musical background would already know and the chances are that if the church has asked you to form and direct a new choir, you have these basic skills. In any case, these explanations can perhaps assist the choir members to understand what the musical shorthand is all about. Just as with anything in life, once we understand it, it isn't nearly as intimidating.

Now that we have discussed the directions for the music, how does the information get communicated from director to singers? How do we know how to direct the beats? There are two or three easy patterns, that when practiced, can take you through the music and help you to resemble a professional. Here they are:

Conducting in 2 (2/4, 2/2, etc.)—2 beats to a measure:

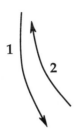

Conducting in 3 (3/4, 3/8, etc.)—3 beats to a measure:

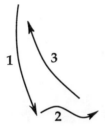

Conducting in 4 (4/4, 4/8, etc.)—4 beats to a measure:

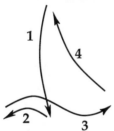

Conducting in 6 (6/8, 6/4, etc.)—6 beats to a measure:

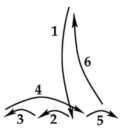

An additional point about 6/8: While slow pieces written in 6/8 tempo may be directed with the above beat pattern, often pieces with this time indication are conducted using only two beats, one for each of the divisions of three. In other words, if you try conducting "It Came Upon the Midnight Clear" with six full beats to a measure, as per the first example above, you will find you're very busy!

Besides, the beats will have to be done quickly. Try it. Can you see how directing this piece in this way is somewhat disturbing in that it is out of character with the song itself? This carol is tranquil and creates a feeling of midnight serenity. It requires direction that does not disturb the mood established by the music and the text. Therefore, most people would direct it with simply a downbeat followed by an upbeat.

When you do this yourself, can you tell the difference in the kind of message you are giving the choir by using the simpler approach? Conducting with two beats retains the calm of this beautiful Christmas carol and at the same time is much easier on the conductor!

With any anthem, generally, we need to pay attention to the mood of the music and words. To direct a piece like "Jingle Bells" with large sweeping beats would be ridiculous, while the great "Hallelujah!" from Handel's *Messiah* can hardly be conducted with tiny beats—not that all of this isn't done. However, the singers rely on the choir director to lead the way, and anything directors can give to preserve the character and concept of a composition is valuable. We have not been given carte blanche to do as we will, for—in some cases—we have tradition to learn from. However, we must listen to our inner voice as musical people; we need to spend time with the music alone to become acquainted with it, whether it is a four part anthem or a hymn that will be sung in unison. This homework can pay dividends and prevent frustration.

The basic beat patterns just explained make it clear to the choir where the *downbeat* is (the initial strong downward movement of the arm) as well as the other beats of the measure. *Keep the forearm fairly firm* when making these beats, but not stiff to the point of directing like a robot. Each conductor has his or her own unique style so it isn't necessary to do it exactly as someone else does. Even if you do not have all the beats clearly delineated, concentrate on the *downbeat*, the first beat of the measure; make it definite. The technique of beating time will gradually become easier with some practice, and can be refined so that you feel comfortable doing it your own way. Play a recording of a hymn or anthem and practice beating time in front of a mirror. Critique yourself. I know a fine song leader and choir director who taught herself this way.

If you have ever watched some of today's leading symphony conductors, you know that with some, the beat is precise, orderly, and completely clear. With others it is hard to find any definite beat whatsoever, even a downbeat. This proves my point that style is completely personal; even the finest musicians often fall short in the area of conducting technique. They, however, are working with professionals whereas we are concerned with the amateur church choir. So for us, the clearer the better.

These volunteers who generously devote their time, energy and talent deserve the best that is in us as choir directors. We need to prepare ourselves to the best of our ability. While we may not be ready to take on the New York Philharmonic Orchestra, we can be ready each week to give our full attention to the choir practice at hand, doing what we have agreed to do. This is our commitment. We can apply ourselves to God's perfect presence and allow God to do the work through us.

9. ALL THINGS WORK TOGETHER FOR GOOD

One of the most helpful things in planning music for the Sunday service is knowing what will happen in other areas of the worship service. For example, what will the Scripture lessons be? What will the minister be speaking about? Is it a special day in the life of the church? Is it a holiday or national day? Will there be any acknowledgments or awards? Will anything take place that might call for particular music? Of course, the best way to have the answers to these questions is to meet with the people involved in planning the Sunday service.

In many churches there is a weekly planning session or staff meeting that includes the minister, assistant/associate minister if any, the youth director, choir director, organist/pianist, and anyone else who needs to be involved. The discussions that develop from these times can produce a coordinated, well thought out service rich in blessings for everyone. In the small church this type of planning is not always possible, but it is possible to have a service that works, which reflects the fact that each person has been aware of what others are doing.

There needs to be communication among people. Usually the minister has his or her Biblical text in mind at least some days in advance and perhaps has some idea of what the sermon will deal with. Even if the scriptures are all the choir director has to go on, that can be a great help in planning the music. It stands to reason that the longer the advance notice, the better the planning. Usually if the choir is working diligently, it will be practicing anthems well before the date they will be sung; after all, a certain amount of time is required to learn the pieces. If there is an anthem the choir has sung in the past that is appropriate for a service, it isn't too difficult to dust it off in a relatively short time. But any choir needs adequate rehearsal to prepare new music. Most choirs sing one anthem each Sunday and that *can* be a hymn. I recommend that the choir director pay attention to what the group is really capable of accomplishing; it is good to challenge people, but be realistic. It is better to sing one thing well each week than to do a mediocre job on two anthems. There are choirs that prefer to sing twice a month (one or two anthems) and let the other Sundays be for soloists from the choir, other talented singers, or instrumentalists in the congregation or community. This is a wonderful way to educate the congregation musically, as it could be an opportunity for people to hear good music performed live if there are not many musical events offered close by. In any case it is desirable to plan selections to coincide with other parts of the service.

I like to obtain the scripture lessons from the minister for a period of one to two months in advance when possible, then find out if there are special happenings being planned by the Sunday school, youth fellowship, Men's/Women's groups, and so forth, to help in scheduling music. The holiday times of the year usually fall into place easily; Christmas, Easter, Thanksgiving are occasions for which many hymns have been written, and it is fairly simple to plan the music.

Check to see if your hymnal has an index that lists hymns under headings such as love, praise, brotherhood, and service. This gives you immediate help in choosing hymns. Spend some time with the texts of the hymns; they offer additional assistance in coordinating music and the rest of the service. I have attended churches where I have wondered if the minister and choir director were even on speaking terms—much less working together on the service—because the hymns did not have any connection to the sermon topic, the Scripture lessons for the day, or anything else. Why not blend all the elements? The effect can be powerful and inspirational.

Because hymnals vary from church to church, I am not going to suggest specific hymns as my personal favorites, but if you have not already done so, become well acquainted with your hymnal. If it has a metrical index you can easily use words with various hymn tunes as long as the meter is the same. For example: "O God, Our Help in Ages Past" is usually sung to the hymn tune "St. Anne," but there are a number of texts that will fit. The metrical guide in this hymn is 8.6.8.6 There are eight syllables in the first line, six in the next; eight in the third line, and six in the last. Another text that can be sung to "St. Anne" is "Praise to the Holiest in the Height." If the meter is right, the text will work with the hymn tune.

Let us take another, perhaps more familiar tune, "Old Hundredth," or what we usually think of as the "Doxology" tune. The meter is 8.8.8.8, sometimes called long meter. Any text with this metrical pattern can be sung to "Old Hundredth." You can begin to see how it works and how you can have some immediate success in introducing new words; the congregation does not have to worry about new words and a new tune at the same time. Spend time browsing through hymns and comparing meters; notice which ones have the same number of syllables and sing through them to see how the words match a different melody. When you find a text that is appropriate for a particular Sunday, type the words and include the typed page in the Sunday bulletins. The organist or pianist can play the old standby tune. The congregation will learn something new in an easy way and the hymn will contribute something meaningful to the service.

A word about protecting copyright. Many of the grand old hymns in our hymnals are in the public domain. This means that we can copy lyrics and/or music without seeking permission from copyright holders. However, if a hymn or song is currently protected by a copyright, one must receive permission from the copyright holder in order to reprint the words or music. How can you tell? Page through your hymnal. If there is a copyright notice at the bottom of the hymn, it may not be reprinted without permission. If there is no such notice, you may feel free to copy as needed.

While on the subject of hymns, I need to say that all too often it is a temptation to sing the same old hymns from month to month. People will simply stop singing on new hymns, feeling they just cannot manage it. Here is a suggestion: Choose a New Hymn of the Month. On the first Sunday you use it, have the choir sing it as an anthem or introit, and include a note in the bulletin telling folks that it will be sung on the next three Sundays by both the choir and congregation. The choir can sing it through once each Sunday before the congregation joins in. It is a wonderful way to introduce new hymns; nobody needs to feel frustrated in struggling through it, and usually by the end of the month the congregation more or less has a new hymn under their belts. This is another situation where the choir can act as worship leaders.

Some churches have begun to use praise choruses in their services, and I have no objection to this as long as the hymns are still sung. Recently in a workshop I led, one participant was a talented fourteen-year-old alto who had grown up in the church and was a very good sight reader and singer. The day after the workshop I led the workshop singers in a community concert that began with an informal hymn-sing, after which I learned that this young singer had never sung—had never even heard of—"The Church's One Foundation." So, if praise choruses are used, I would urge you not to abandon or ignore the marvelous hymns that are part of the Christian church's heritage.

Make up a typical Sunday service, to show how the music can work with everything else to provide a time of beauty, inspiration, and worshipful praise. It is a Sunday in late July, in the long season of Trinity. The service will honor Faith Fuller, who has served the church for fifty years in various capacities—Sunday school teacher, pianist for the junior choir, office volunteer, stewardship committee member, circle member, coffee hour hostess, and numerous other things. There is to be a plaque presented to Faith during the service, acknowledging her extraordinary devotion and expressing the thanks of the congregation. The minister is using (as the lectionary suggests) James 2: 18-26, (faith and works), preceded by an appropriate Old Testament scripture. The order of service might look something like this:

Processional Hymn—"When Morning Gilds the Skies"

Call to Worship/Invocation

Greeting followed by announcements and award

Hymn—"Faith of Our Fathers"

The Old Testament Lesson

The New Testament Lesson

Prayers

Anthem—"Take My Life and Let It Be"
(1st vs.—unison choir, 2nd vs.—soprano solo, 3rd vs.—baritone solo, 4th vs.—choir in harmony)

Offertory
Invitation/Hymn of Commitment—"Breathe on
  Me, Breath of God"
Benediction
Closing (Recessional) Hymn—"O God, Our Help
  in Ages Past"

For the anthem the choir director would
undoubtedly make a choice based on what the
choir is prepared to sing. In this case, it is late
summer, not every choir member is in town due to
vacations, and the director has decided to use a
perfectly suited hymn. By using soloists and having
the choir sing in unison and then in harmony, it
serves in the same manner as an octavo anthem.
All the hymns have been chosen with the special
occasion, scriptures, and sermon in mind, and
everything adds up to a memorable Sunday for
Faith Fuller and all others present.

Naturally, this is only one possibility; the point is
to coordinate various aspects of the service. Very
little effort is required to do this and the results
are well worth it.

Sometimes it works well to tailor hymn texts to
an occasion. Often there is at least one person in
the choir who loves to write and who has the
ability to make a line scan well. In the case of
Faith Fuller's being acknowledged for her service
to the church, it would personalize the proceedings
to have a verse or two of a familiar hymn tune
with words celebrating Faith and her contribution
to the church. A gentle, loving tribute done with a
light touch can mean a lot to the person being
celebrated; the honoree will remember it fondly
while it underscores the appreciation being ex-
pressed.

If the hymn tune is in the public domain, there
is no problem about including the hymn tune with
personalized text in the Sunday bulletin. If the
tune is not in the public domain, permission needs
to be obtained from the copyright holder.

METRICAL INDEX

SM (66.86)
BOYLSTON 413
DENNIS 553, 557
FESTAL SONG 129, 576
ST. MICHAEL 372, 388, 662, 730
ST. THOMAS 540, 732
SUTTON COMMON 262
TRENTHAM 420

SM with Refrain
MARCHING TO ZION 733
MARION 160
VINEYARD HAVEN 161

SMD (66.86 D)
BEALOTH 332
DIADEMATA 88, 327, 421, 513
TERRA BEATA 111, 144

CM (86.86)
AMAZING GRACE 378
ARLINGTON 511
ARMENIA 554
AZMON 57, 59, 422, 608

CAMPMEETING 492
CHRISTMAS 236
CORONATION 154
CRIMOND 118, 136
DETROIT 390
DIADEM 155
DOVE OF PEACE 617
EVAN 566
GRÄFENBERG 193, 266
LAND OF REST 269, 613, 695
McKEE 548
MAITLAND 424
MARSH CHAPEL 426, 551
MARTYRDOM 294
MORNING SONG 198, 226
RICHMOND 417
ST. AGNES 175, 445, 561
ST. ANNE 117
ST. MAGNUS 326
ST. PETER 549
TWENTY-FOURTH 658
WINCHESTER OLD 470, 603

CM with Repeat
ANTIOCH 246
CM with Refrain
EL NATHAN 714
GIFT OF FINEST WHEAT 629
HUDSON 359
McAFEE 472
MARTIN 130

INDEX OF TOPICS AND CATEGORIES
Italic type indicates poetry and prayers
Psalms without reference numbers are found in the Psalter, pages 738-862

ADORATION AND PRAISE 57-152. *Also:*
280 All glory, laud, and honor
554 All praise to our redeeming Lord
553 And are we yet alive
675 As the sun doth daily rise
199 Canticle of Mary
684 Christ, mighty Savior
260 Christ, upon the mountain peak
411 Dear Lord, lead me day by day
612 Deck thyself, my soul, with gladness
711 For all the saints
705 *For Direction*
477 *For Illumination*
731 Glorious things of thee are spoken
660 God is here
325 Hail, thou once despised Jesus
478 Jaya ho jaya ho
718 Lo, he comes with clouds descending
498 My prayer rises to heaven
198 My soul gives glory to my God
686 O gladsome light
267 O love, how deep, how broad
727 O what their joy and their glory must be
258 O wondrous sight! O vision fair
248 On this day earth shall ring
604 Praise and thanksgiving be to God
715 Rejoice, the Lord is King

348 Softly and tenderly Jesus is calling
347 Spirit Song
374 Standing on the promises
375 There is a balm in Gilead
380 There's within my heart a melody
525 We'll Understand It Better By and By
526 What a friend we have in Jesus

ALDERSGATE
363 And can it be that I should gain
550 Christ, from whom all blessings flow
603 Come, Holy Ghost, our hearts inspire
651 Come, Holy Ghost, our souls inspire
386 Come, O thou Traveler unknown
387 *Come, O thou Traveler unknown*
58 *Glory to God, and praise and love*
59 *Mil voces*
57 O for a thousand tongues to sing
515 Out of the depths I cry to you
342 *Where shall my wondering soul begin*

ALL SAINTS DAY. *See* **Christian Year**

AMENS 897-904

ANNIVERSARIES. *See* **Church Anniversaries; Heritage**

ASCENSION. *See* **Christian Year**

10. SING AND REJOICE

If there is a choir before you assume leadership, no doubt there is some music available and a choir library, whether large or small. If that is the case, then there will be some music for the choir to work on. But if you do not like any of the pieces, or if none of them are right for the group you are beginning to work with, you will want to be thinking about new possibilities. If you have been asked to organize a choir from scratch, there probably isn't anything to draw on and everything must be acquired.

Do not overlook the value of hymns. They can be sung with much variety, such as solo verses by just men, just women, in unison, or in harmony. It also makes sense that the group would want to get busy on some real anthems to challenge themselves and to function in their roles as worship leaders by continuing to grow musically. In any situation, if we are not growing, then we are not fully alive.

Where to start?

If you have a music store in your area that handles choral music, you are especially blessed. Go and spend some time browsing through the shelves to see what is available and what you feel you and your choir can master. If there isn't such a place near you in which to shop, keep reading for other alternatives.

First, I think it is important that the singers have some immediate wins, that they work on challenging pieces that can also be mastered. There is an enormous number of choir anthems on the market today, anthems that range from very easy to very hard. But more important than the degree of difficulty or number of pieces learned is the quality of the music. If I am going to ask a group of people to invest their valuable time learning something, it might as well be—it had better be—something that has musical value. Of course, it is up to directors to select choir music. Probably no two would agree completely about what are the best pieces for a choir at any stage of its development. Everyone has to go with his or her own preferences and the ability of the choir.

As a musician, my first love is the classic choral repertory. I have always used music by Mozart, J.S. Bach, Mendelssohn, and other great choral composers. Yes, this has been with volunteer, non-professional choirs and ensembles. My experience has been that when the music is first handed out,

there might be a few comments or groans about classical music, but once the piece is learned, the singers love it.

In one particular choir I directed, at least one-third of the members had never sung in a choir previously and/or did not read music. I chose the "Domine Fili" from Vivaldi's "Gloria," which is not terribly difficult as far as notes are concerned. The singers thought at first reading that it would be impossible, as it was classical, and in Latin, but by the time they had learned it, it was their favorite thing. Anytime we had a few moments left at the close of rehearsal, they asked to sing it. The same happened with "Sicut Locutus Est" from the Bach "Magnificat," also in Latin. I am not suggesting that a brand new choir tackle these particular anthems. What I am saying is that people love to be challenged and they appreciate the inherent quality—the beauty and genius—of the music.

There are many simple anthems available in which both the music and the text are well-written. Unfortunately, there are also too many that are what I call "fluff," pieces that offer no real challenge to the choir and that are boring musically. I suspect directors sometimes use these because they feel insecure in attempting to direct something more musically demanding, not because they are the only pieces the choir can manage.

A very simple anthem can be challenging, interesting, and beautiful; it does not have to knock everybody out with a lot of notes sung as fast as possible. Often the real challenge lies in singing the piece with great intensity, or singing long legato phrases, or attaining a good blend of voices, or singing a capella—on pitch. I believe one of the most beautiful pieces of choral music ever written, and certainly one that is a challenge to sing well, is Mozart's "Ave Verum Corpus," forty-six measures of musical perfection and deep feeling. It is marked "Adagio," the notes are fairly easy to learn, but it also changes keys and has elements of counterpoint, all of which make it interesting to learn and a sheer joy to perform and to hear. Again, I am not recommending that you rush out to buy this for your choir, but they certainly can work toward being able to do it by working on music of quality that demands their best effort.

Another rich field to explore is the traditional. Folk music and spirituals are a part of our history and musical heritage in the United States. There also is a wealth of traditional music from other countries. There are wonderful arrangements available of many spirituals and a wide variety of folk songs whose words are spiritually directed. I have found that singers love to sing these pieces, as most speak to the heart and evoke warm response in the singers and those who listen.

There are many good settings of biblical texts in contemporary arrangements on the market. In addition, some fine arrangers are at work, doing settings of some of the spirituals and folk tunes that are wonderfully rhythmic—often using a lot of syncopation, clapping, and spoken phrases. However, highly syncopated music is demanding and the fledgling choir is apt to find it frustrating. Give them some time before tackling these, unless the syncopation is so obvious that it cannot be missed. On these pieces, it is essential the director be well prepared, and that he or she has the rhythmic patterns down pat in order to teach the choir. In my case, because teaching syncopation has never been my strong suit, I have always worked quite a while on a syncopated piece before I ever present it to the group. The investment always pays off.

Now, what if there is no place to buy music where you are? Do not worry, all is not lost. One of the best ways to have access to choir music if you do not have a library at your church is to talk to choir directors of other churches and choirs. Other directors are usually very happy to share and to be of service. After all, isn't this the essence of our Christian faith?

Many music publishers send out information about their new releases to churches all over the country, whether there is a choir or not. If your church is on their mailing lists and you receive such notices, look them over carefully. These notices let you know what is being published, and you could find something that would work well for your choir. Also, take note of music listed on the covers of anthems you do use. Most of the major publishers include listings of available anthems, not necessarily just recent things, that are standards in their publishing library.

You can also write to publishers and request a catalog. If you used something you liked, and that your choir responded to in a positive way, there are probably more anthems where that one came from. If you hear a group perform an anthem that appeals to you, try to find out what edition it is, who published it, and where to write or call for it. You need not be concerned about having enough music; you and the music will find each other.

It is a great time to be making music. There is so much to choose from. When we think of the years gone by, when music had to be hand copied, when the only way one could hear music (short of attending a concert) was to perform it personally, we obviously have much to be thankful for.

Beyond the availability of all kinds of music in our age, we need to take time to marvel at the incredible gift of the human voice. How magnificent that it comes in four basic categories—soprano, alto, tenor and bass—and that no two voices are identical. How generous of God to allow us such infinite variety in this Divine Instrument. Let us remember, as choir people, to be "filled with the Spirit," speaking in psalms, hymns, and spiritual songs, singing and making melody in our hearts (Ephesians 5:18-19, NIV).

11. THEN THOU SHALT HAVE GOOD SUCCESS

From the first time the choir meets, it is important to be clear about what is involved in being a choir member and what is expected. These decisions are not strict, authoritarian rules given by the person conducting. Rather, they are a few guidelines that will contribute to good performance of music and that will make everybody's participation less stressful. Perhaps the following pointers would be thought obvious, but I consider them essential for the successful choir.

The choir needs to watch the director. It is surprising to watch some church choirs get up to sing on Sunday morning and see pairs of eyes taking in everything and everybody in the sanctuary *except* the choir director! I have even seen singers wave at people in the congregation, wink, or mouth a silent message. The other extreme is the choir member who buries his or her face in the music and whose eyes are never seen again for the duration of the anthem. The only place anyone needs to direct attention to is the director—whether that be in front of the group, or at the organ or piano.

The communication lines must continually stay open to ensure that everyone is together and all are functioning as One. Isn't that what the choir does? It is a number of people singing as one instrument with somebody assuming the role of director. The director has the responsibility to direct—impossible to do if individuals are not watching. There are moments when having one's eyes fastened on the choir director can save a piece of music from disaster: if singers come in too soon or too late, if the tempo gets out of hand, if something happens in the accompaniment, and on and on.

I encourage choirs to memorize their music as much as possible. Yes, I know this sounds like a large order and possibly an intimidating prospect. But after the choir has worked on a piece for a number of weeks, it is fairly safe to assume that a good deal of the music is already memorized, though singers might not realize it.

Challenge the choir. Ask them to sing a piece they have been practicing for awhile without the music. Make it clear that nobody will be asked to leave if they cannot make it all the way through—it is just to see what they can do. The singers are generally surprised that they can do more than they thought. The music is often the thing that comes between the choir and the choir director.

When music is committed to memory, there is nothing in the way of perfect communication; there is no need to divide one's attention between the printed page and the director's instructions. Singers are completely free to focus entirely on the director. If the director chooses not to use the music, so much the better, as it leaves him or her free to focus entirely on the choir and the job at hand. But be sure to know the score.

On Sunday morning there needs to be a warm up session before the service. This needs to be a period of at least thirty minutes, as by the time a few vocalizing exercises are completed, it leaves little more than twenty minutes for last minute brush up on the anthem for the day. This time is valuable to choir and director as it can refresh people on particular details. Usually choirs rehearse in the middle of the week, Wednesday or Thursday night, and it can be a long time until Sunday morning. The warm-up period offers an opportunity to go over tricky passages, to review entrances, cut-offs, all the things that make for good choral singing. The choir member's commitment should include this Sunday morning time.

Of course, you already know my rule: only the singers who attended choir practice are involved in this review of the day's anthem. In my choirs, anyone who does not rehearse during the week should not sing the anthem on Sunday, though they are welcome to sing the service music and hymns with the choir. If it is decided that the Sunday warm-up time is forty-five minutes to an hour long, there is an argument to be made for the fact that someone who missed choir practice could possibly become adequately prepared to sing the anthem. This is probably the case, but there is still the issue of singers' commitment to attend choir practice and the issue of fairness to those who did attend. Unless the choir members feel strongly that they want this as their policy, I do not think it is a good idea.

A choir that watches the director like a pilot watches the instrument panel is a choir that sings as one voice. The Sunday morning warm up session, with all choir members present at the agreed upon time is an opportunity to iron out last minute problems in the anthem. These commitments and agreements build excellent musicianship in the choir, help each member grow in responsibility, and create a joyful discipline from which great singing can be born.

12. THY KINGDOM COME
(A Very Personal Note . . .)

In looking over the things touched on in the preceding pages, I hope the resonating chord is that of love. The strong glue that will bind people together, that will allow them to become a successful choir is love. For years I directed choirs without fully realizing the truth of this statement—I would work very hard in attempts to bring singers together in ways that encouraged them to sing well, to do their best, and to be an accomplished choir. Sometimes they did all of these things, but there was no sense of connectedness—individuals would still skip rehearsals, drop out for awhile (always with good reason), and at such times I confess I was at a loss to know why. I loved what I was doing; I loved making music, serving in God's house. I knew they loved being part of the choir during the times we had done well, but I wondered, "Where is their sense of commitment?" I had to consider that perhaps it was me, that the people in the choir did not enjoy my leadership enough to keep an agreement to be present. I went through many times of self-doubt and discouragement, searching for the answer to make it work.

I never felt comfortable in saying, "That's the way it is with volunteer choirs; they show up when it's convenient." However, for a long time I did not understand what the missing ingredient was. I went through periods of feeling alternately excited about the choir and its progress, and depressed because I did not feel that we were what a choir should be. I did not realize that as the leader, it was up to me to set the tone for the group; they needed to make agreements and their own decisions, while I needed to understand my role as director. I gradually started to grasp the fact that as the leader, I had to call the choir to its highest (to serve God, not me or the church, as a member of the choir), to expect them to give their word and to keep it, and to be faithful. It began to dawn on me that I had been timid in taking the lead, in letting them know what was expected of them. I began to see clearly that the choir could function in a completely new and different way if I were willing to be completely honest about what I wanted from the choir members, not worrying about what it might do to my popularity, and if somehow our rehearsals could become times when people felt appreciated. It could make a difference if they felt appreciated and loved by me and by their fellow choir members. It could make a difference if they felt appreciated not only for their voices, but because of who they are . . . and whose they are.

Seeing all of us in the choir as children of the One God, desiring to serve, I began to open myself more and more in appreciation of the singers who were devoting their valuable time each week. I began to see myself as a learner, just as the choir was. While it was true that I stood in front of them directing the music, I began to see that we were all learning valuable lessons about service and love in an area we had chosen because of our particular God-given talents, abilities, and/or preparation. I started to ask myself (and God) how could we as a choir serve best as worship leaders? How could we share ourselves with the congregation in such a way as to aid in establishing love as our first priority?

Unfortunately, all of these realizations did not occur during my tenure with one choir, but developed over a protracted period during which I grew in my spiritual life. I learned more about what it might mean to be a human being. I have often felt that I would like to apologize to all the wonderful people who have been part of various choirs I directed before coming to these new realizations. However, it is never productive to lament "what might have been," so I can only be thankful that I have learned a few things about working with people, trusting that those persons will understand that I was honestly doing the best I knew how to do at the time.

At any rate, at a certain point the pianist/organist, the choir president, and I began to make sure that love was the focus of our choir time. We began to implement the things I have talked about in this book, always keeping in mind the privilege it is to serve, to praise, and worship God through music. With the singers, we created an atmosphere of joy at our rehearsals; we worked hard on our music, we set up choir meetings to socialize and to plan projects such as serving breakfast to the congregation once a month, asking only a small charge that subsidized our having choir outfits made. We consciously made efforts to greet people we had not seen in church before, or those who might have been away or ill. We asked newcomers if they might be interested in joining the choir. Many did, as they were drawn to the joyful enthusiasm of the choir members.

We divided our choir year in half—and at the beginning of each part (September and January) we had an "Intensive Weekend," during which we sang through all the music that was to be done in that period, brought in resource people to teach and inspire us, consumed enormous quantities of delicious pot luck food, and experienced warm times of personal sharing with each other. At the conclusion of the weekend, I asked for the individual commitment of each person who intended to sing with the choir that term. Yes, I asked for a verbal "Yes, I'm committing to the choir for this term." That became the first step of our becoming a choir family and throughout the ensuing weeks strong bonds of love developed among all of us. The congregation noticed and began to share in

our enthusiasm. We sang in neighboring communities and we gave concerts once or twice a year. At least one quarter of the sixty-five member group had never sung in a choir before or did not read music. One or two had worked in music semi-professionally, but most fell into the middle in terms of choir experience. If I had never known it before, I learned then that truly "the greatest of these is love." We had lived the transforming experience of love within the choir.

When I have talked with choir people (directors and singers) about their particular problems (having enough people, inconsistent attendance, etc), I have always urged them to work first to establish a safe, loving place for singers, and often I cannot help noticing they have tuned out. After all, it does not make much practical sense. Shouldn't the music come first? How can you sing anthems if there aren't enough people? What about getting people with really good voices who can read music? Let's not forget we have been told clearly to seek the kingdom *first* and all else will follow. It was years before I finally awakened to this principle where the choir is concerned. What is the kingdom of God if it is not love? Why should choirs be any different from anything else? Build a community of love in your choir and watch the miracles happen.

A FOOTNOTE

As time goes by undoubtedly you, as choir director, will probably want to attend workshops, seminars, or other such endeavors to continue to broaden your learning and expertise. Of course, as you do this, it can be taken back to the choir to allow them to grow, too. Sometimes there are opportunities for choir directors and singers to participate together, which is the best of all in my opinion.

Read available material (articles, books, magazines) about choirs and choral goings-on. You do not have to agree with all of it. Find out what works best for you and your group. Browse in bookstores to see what is being written that could possibly be helpful. Watch other directors—professional and amateur. Again, you do not need to imitate them, but see what techniques they are using. I assure you that occasionally, in this way, you will learn what you don't want to do!

We have a unique opportunity as choir directors to assist others to be in touch with one of the most beautiful parts of being alive, the indescribable delight of music. Music touches us at our deepest level, bypassing all our intellectual processes. With music we can feel fully alive in every sense; we can be joyful, sad, hopeful, and inspired. Every aspect of life can be experienced to some degree through music. As we learn more and more about ourselves with those in the choir, then we give of ourSelves. We give of our God-given talent and while we may tend to think we are not overly endowed with great musical ability, we can do what we have been created and called to do: We can serve. Jesus was ever the servant; he gave us the example and many years ago the great American writer Henry Wadsworth Longfellow wrote words that are a strong reminder:

**"Give what you have.
To someone it may be better than you dare to think."**

ABOUT THE AUTHOR

Jean Anderson lives in Seattle, Washington. A graduate of Florida State University, she majored in Music Education. In addition to teaching music in public schools and doing music therapy with the mentally ill, she has directed choirs in churches of several denominations.

Currently Jean Anderson conducts ecumenical choral workshops all over the United States, and leads singing for camps, conferences, and retreats.

She is also a lyricist, and has written the words to many anthems, hymns, choruses, and songs.

For further information about her choral workshops and music, please contact:

AmaDeus Group
Route 1, Box 241
Walla Walla, Washington 99362